Incoherence:
It is so confusing to be young

E. P. Johnson

Forward:

At this moment, I feel nothing but confused. And there's
nothing wrong with that. Confusion can be the telescope
peering down the rabbit hole or it can be the hope to survive.
I'm doing the best that I can and yet I find myself so lost. I have
a feeling you might be feeling it too. So let yourself be young
and hopeful, whomever you are in this moment.

So, here I am. Read ahead, hold my hand and we will walk
together through confusion. Life is either the great abyss or the
great oyster and most of the time we feel in the middle. When
people talk about life being gray they talk of the boredom or
avoidance of their inner voice.

And every time the sun sets I think, *I should be outside.*

Yours Honestly,

E. P. Johnson

Part 1: Where I've Been

Part 2: Where I'm Going

Part 3: Who I am not

Part I
Where I've Been

Haunted
Messy
...but growing

The four walls that keep me safe
Are the same ones that entrap me
As my brain floats in the safety of my skull
I float in the safety of my apartment
The ceiling swirls
And I feel blind
The carpet feels like sandpaper
My back wilts from looking at a screen
I fold into myself
And die a human origami
Before exploding into dust

And in the depths
Of my shadows
I saw a dark silhouette
Of doubt and fear
Their faces are ugly
Ripped to shreds
Skin dripping away
Bones poking through
Eyes gripped to mine
Looking for something
To hold

You're not hungry
But you're not not hungry
So you eat
You're not tired
But you're not not tired
So you sleep
You're not horny
But you're not not horny
So you masturbate
You're not lonely
But you're not not lonely
So you facetime a friend
You're not bored
But you're not not bored
So you wallow
And pray for death
Eat something
And go back to sleep

Hold me
Like you could ever love me
Squeeze me
Until my doubts have been pushed through my mouth
Kiss my hand
Like you won't treat me like a stranger
Stroke my hair
As if I'm still capable of love
And then run
Run fast; run without looking back
Because it's easier to walk away
When you don't have someone pulling you back in

I can't
I can't
        finish this sentence
It's like motivation
Is across the hall
And my legs won't move
Not for lack of trying
Not for lack of wanting
To move and to be

But rather that there's no point

In wasting
        energy that's not there

Youth isn't wasted on the young
Rather
Joy is wasted on those who are grown
Eluded by the emotions we cannot grasp
The pain we are taught to swallow
And all the little moments that never met our enormous hopes
Dreams crushed by larger reality
The stars and moon sucked into the basking abyss
And my hope dying with the earth I call home

Even driving to the grocery store
Feels like freedom
There's nothing like listening to the radio
Rolling down the windows
And feeling like it's all okay
Like I might have a busy week again
That I could go get a drink at a bar
That we may ever see
The world return to *normal*
And then we pull up to the grocery store
And see masks
And the shuffle of fear
Cart full of toilet paper and water bottles
And reality sets like the sun

Loving you was soul crushing
Because you loved me
When I was incapable of happiness
Anhedoniac
You loved the sad girl you saw within me
You loved the little bird with broken wings
You loved the strong man you thought you could be
But all you did
Was love a sad girl
Who couldn't be happy
for you
Unfixable
So you deserted her
And became the little bird with broken wings
Who you couldn't save
We became alone
Alone and broken

Sorry I didn't reply to your text
The fog over my brain
Has now covered my eyes
It is too thick to see through
And now I fear that all I can see is the light of the sun
Peeking through the ashy haze
Like a headlight in the dark
And who knows if the light will come back

Who knows if I will come back

Society beat me with the responsibility stick
And now I have no joy
No fun
And no reason to move forward

Where can I be in the company of the wild?

I want to meet people who are free
Who still choose to feel the wind on their skin
And do stupid things for love
Defy doubt
Lean into hope for the future

Instead of people like me

Who rolled over and took it
And worry about taxes, rent, and career mobility
Let me live in the day
May the sun guide me again!

Love is patient
Love is kind
Bitter
and cruel
When I feel bad
I kowtow to you
You don't realize
That our fate is doom
Despite being full of love
Your heart had no room

The willow loved the water
Rooted in the river
Stubborn was the willow
Bumping along the river
Trying to grow within
The gushing rapids
Couldn't grasp
Where the current swept
Trapped until she reached the water's edge
She found the tender soil
And the water within
Ready to take hold

Ego at the center
Sadness rests on the heart
I reach out my long, frail arm to hold you
And the cracks show on my body
Alone I am protected again
Longing to be close to be someone
Who wants to look into my eyes forever
Whose willing to hold my hand when my skin turns to tissue
paper
And heart flutters
To behold what we've grown together

Delude me
The way I used to delude myself
That loving someone who couldn't love me back
Was fine
Not just fine
But good
That it felt good
Actually it was as good as it gets
Was the greatest lie I ever told
And I told it to myself
Over and over again
Until everything I had
Was gone
And I was empty
Loveless, like you

There is nothing more painful
Than the obligation of familial love
It lacks the honesty
That allows the identity to exist
As I smile and hug you
My grin covers the lies in saccharin
My body melts
Into the nothingness
I feel
In your presence

The nape of your neck
Is the loneliest place I could be
Loving you
Made me miss Him

Ringing in my ear
Unwelcome
The greeting of a man
Testing me
Would I crack?
Or would I walk calmly away
As if I were going somewhere
Without a care in the world
My smirk grows wider
My ponytail pulls tighter
Pace hastens

I can tell you loads on dating
But nothing of relationships
I know sex
Not intimacy
Lust and I know each other well
But love and I only met once
I know others
But so little about myself
So don't take my advice
Because I don't really know anything

Lost Angeles
It's not what you know
It's who you've slept with
Where business
Is strictly pleasure
Shook me up
Turned this sweet loving girl
A cold, clever bitch

I'm crying over a guy
Whom I don't miss anymore
Because the feelings of longing
Are more pleasant
Than the creeping loneliness
Of the cobwebs of my cold dead heart
Incapable of loving again

The ugliest part about sadness
Is the years and years of choices
That lead me to the path of unhappiness
I lean my head back
And baptize myself
In tears of self hatred
And bask in the sadness
I chose again

Part II
Where I'm Going

Perplexed
Where am I?
Here
...I guess

The innermost being is the dancer
Moves with sound
Who sets fear free
Brings light to truth
That we are all sprite beings
Looking to plie as one
Merge with the noise
Tiptoe the web

I miss traffic.

I miss that all of us had somewhere to be
That over this stretch of highway
Was a job to be done
A task to be finished
A day to be had
It's the same way that I miss the sun
Because morning never comes
Because morning can't start
Unless there's something to do
Somewhere to be
And a reason to be awake

The poetry of my heart
Is as broken as the language I speak
I watch my beloved art form
Fall flat
At the expense of what could be
I have run out of words to express
All the anguish I feel

The numbers of today
Rumble around in my brain
As I long to distance myself from reality
But the truth
Is that the distraction is only as good as the death rate
And as the dead keep adding
My brain refocuses
And fears the never ending
Effects
For my already depressed generation

The man in the red jacket
Looked at me through the morning fog
Eyes meet
He didn't smile
He nodded once
Among the salt and the grey sea
I believed in myself
Stole the first boat I saw
And sailed toward the nod

More contagious than this
Is the paranoia
I've lost countless friends
And family already
They're dropping all around me
I can smell the fear as I pass neighbors in the street
As my friends stopped hugging me
And public spaces are filled
With people huddled in cars in parking lots
Sending one designated person to support the last standing
small businesses
And the scumbags who buy sanitizer in bulk
Take the last can of beans
And the world keeps
A six foot distance from reality

As a single tear leaks from my eye
The boundaries that took years to build
Dissolve
To the sound of you playing the piano

Time is now a substance
Something I'd like to smoke away
As it oozes from my ears
I remove my wristwatch
My clock is melting
Tuesday has no meaning
Except for the Tuesday I got my $1200
Or was it a Wednesday?
As one day melts into another
It inches so slowly
That I wonder if my day
Of reckoning will ever come
But finals don't wait
Bills don't wait
Debts don't wait
Doom doesn't wait
But time stands still

I think the strangest part
Is listening to my father's voice come from my brother's mouth
Watching my face grow new lines
Looking in the mirror and seeing my mother
Going to more funerals
Watching friends get married
And wondering when my life started

How did it start without me?

Grief is tricky
It's the painful reminder of absence
But the grief I feel is not for absence
It's for the life I used to have
The one I can still see
Out my window
In my photographs
The people who I text
The job that laid me off
That will eventually need me back
But I lost a dream of closeness
Of a world I could give a hug
But now physical touch is nothing but a
Mere threat
Of a deadly disease

My dream is
To live in a lighthouse
Alone to protect the seas
Patrol the night
Walk about the docks
Let the cold wet air
Pour over my skin
And have no one know my name
My dream is
To die an anonymous death
And be swallowed by the water
That I watched over
Live out eternity as seafoam
With the spirits of mermaids
And sailors alike

My world leaders want me dead?
It sure seems like it
The adults are dying
Leaving the youth to wipe the mistakes of our elders

But what example have they set?
That lying and economic interests lead to death
Deaths of individuals
Treated as numbers
It's not personal
How ugly to die a number
I wish they saw our humanity
But what could you expect from greedy old cis white men?
Destruction
War
Genocide
Systemic racism
Oh, and
A global pandemic

The empty cavity in my chest
Has left enough room
For my brain to expand
My mind is hungry for knowledge
But
I truly crave someone to love me
Though I can't love back
But the tiny piece of my heart I have left
Wants to go it alone
So I don't hurt others
The way I've been hurt

I can't look in the mirror
But I don't see myself
I see a figure
A shadow of who I thought I would be
I see a girl fraught with fear
I see the anger I feel at my ravaged world
I see paranoia well up into tears and spill down my cheeks
I see a silent voice
I see my coping mechanism shatter into glass so small
That the sand pours through my fingers
I am barely human today
But my heart is beating
...so I guess I'm okay

Thank you for asking

I will never be as beautiful
As I am today
My body is a fading commodity
I will only be able to use it for manipulation for a short time
longer
But I'm retired
I'm embracing my fine lines
I'm embracing adult acne
And the scars on my legs
There's no one on earth left to impress
So let my biological clock tick away
And when I'm dead
The spiders can have my eyes

Sweet embrace
Your hair
Melting in my fingers
Your cheek
Warms mine
Humbled by your touch

Morning dew
Sits politely on my windshield
Waiting to be swept away
For clarity
When I look out to see
That the clarity
Was always there
I merely swept away
My fragmented distraction

Looking across the vast canyon of my life
Knowing I will get there
But the years I live now
Moves me closer to the edge
Moves me closer to the time
When my future is behind
And my past is ahead

This is God's punishment
For our lack of care to the earth
Humans got greedy
And we couldn't save our planet
So God sent this
To clean us out and keep us home
Long enough
So the birds could nest
Skies could clear
Oceans could heal
Fish could spawn
And when the rain comes
God reminds us to stay in and stay dry
That;
We ultimately did this to ourselves

The touches of light
Along with the green flash
Spill out of my eyes
And into a pool of moonlight
When I fall into the pearly bask
Daydreaming during sunset
Again

I feel so far
From the space I long to be
I can see where I think I'll go
I see the land of expectations
Their love takes me to places I've been
But my love takes me where I want
His love takes me across oceans

I fear not
What I lost from you
I fear the love I gave you
I gave it all to you
But piece by piece
I reclaimed the person I gave to you
Put her together
And reminded her that she can give again
But she won't give what she gave to you
Not another
Not another like you

My life
A plot of land
Like undeveloped property
With only the foundation built
The construction is yet to come
What will I build?
And is it even mine to choose?

I caught a glimpse
Of why I do what I do
You the storyteller
And I the listener
Patiently
Putting a puzzle together
Of the moon that rose
The night you were born
The music you love
Places you've worked
A story
Immortal
Because you had the courage
And I had the honor
Of listening

I'm sorry I can't be that girl
I am now a woman
A woman with dreams
And a repaired heart
A woman well aware of her potential
Full of might and love
Ready to surrender
To curiosity and passion
I'm sorry I can't be that girl
The girl you fuck
The girl who who moves mountains to make sure your coffee is
hot
That your keys are in your pocket
Your emotions are fed
And I can't be that girl
Who you touch when you're lonely
And cry about in private
Who makes you breakfast in bed
And likes every dumb movie you like
I am not that girl
Who entertains your friends
Wears the right dress to your work thing
And writes your mother a birthday card
Because I would never ask you to
I could never ask you to

My hands were warm
My thoughts broke into little pieces and scattered across our
love
You were red
Like my appetite
Satiate the touch of your skin to mine
Let me feel the mountains and valleys in your back
And carve rivers
With the light touch of my index finger
Caress my arm and cheek
Feast on my warmth
My warm hands

My eyes are brought to tears
When I think of the things I've heard
What a joy it's been to hear your story
To writhe in pain with you
And to walk beside you on a path of understanding
The palpable tension in your tired hands
Became mine
When you shared them with me
When they told a story of courage and comfort
Thank you
For sharing yourself
Story by story
I listened

God's perfect love
Will carry me home
In ways yours cannot
And that's not to say
That your love
Isn't desirable
Because it's the only human love
I want
For all of my days

What are the words I will be remembered by?
Were they any good
Or just passing observations
Were they strong words
Or merely exchanged glances
And did they mean anything to you
Did you extrapolate the meaning I tried to convey
Or are all of my memories lost in translation

And yet
So many pages to fill
So little time to occupy
And too many amazing people to meet
Somehow too busy
For coffee
Or a phone call
Just enough time
To write this
And move on

Part III
Who I am not

Unknown
Who?
Not me
Maybe you?

58

Embrace in the sun
Sand beneath our skin
I'm in my minds eye again
Escaping the trap of my daily
In the shadow of the palm
And the warmth of the basking daylight

Being high
Feels pleasant
But does its illusion fool me?
Unfortunately
No.
The same way memories of outside
Taunts us
With the feeling Of being trapped in a bubble
In the past
The taste of my present is bitter
Past lady
I long for you

How bizarre to tell a child to
dream big
To follow the dreams that *we* didn't achieve
The ones we sacrificed
So we could have them
Humans are like Russian dolls
Of lost goals

Giving birth to resentment
Giving birth to resentment
Giving birth to resentment
Giving birth to resentment

I like my nihilism
Like I like my sex
Spoon fed to me
By a sexy stranger
And that's what this virus robbed me of
Conversations in the patios of bars
Sharing a cigarette
With a pseudointellectual
And the ability to turn
My brain off
When the conversation
Turns to our flat earth
Or how I'm so different from the other girls
Quarantine is the hangover
You have in his bed the next
Bitter truth
Force fed

I want to run
Out of my mind
And into the earth
I want to melt into the core of the mother
Who sustains my life
I miss her
Despite her punishment
Despite her hellfire
Raining down on her people
I want to be part of her
But not trapped
Outside of her care
As I am now

I want to get up and run
Run away from it all
Run until I find where the sun sets
Run free with the birds above
Escape the limitations humans have put on ourselves
But I've already been domesticated
It's too late for me
Society has brainwashed me
And I'm left to work an office job and die
Like a caged bird who refuses
To fly
But you
You can still run
Run until you don't think about it anymore
Run until your breath is gone

Hey,
Are you okay?

Please answer honestly
Because if you say "fine" or "good"
I may snap
And choke you through your screen
I want to hear that you're losing your mind

Like me

I feel them touching me
Sometimes I think it's my own hair tickling me
But it's not
The voices in my head are taunting me
Begging to be released
The only time they don't pester me
Is when I put pen to paper
The ghosts that haunt me
Are the reminders that taunt me
Reminding me that I am the only one
Who trapped me
Behind the bars of my life choices
So be free little choices
And stop tapping on my shoulder

I boldly walk to the edge
Without fear
Without hesitation
Gingerly block the blinding light
With my forearm
Feel the edge with my toes
Is this it?
Can I walk back or is this the next stage
The existence of existence
Swallows me whole in a warm light
And I begin to float in the bubble of my mind

I can't take the jump
From here to there
It's my teeth that hold me back
When they're on edge
I take a backseat until my life forces me to go
But every once in a while
We meet someone
Whose on the other side
Who jumped
Like we made the jump
To make it
To where we are now

Germs
Calisthenics
Anger
Betrayal
Hot cereal
Niche
Summer day
Poker
Joe Camel
Waste basket
Paper plane
Death hotel
Child
Light
Hail
Bed
It was a strange dream
Rather a daydream
More like a day I had
That I experienced in a reality
I've yet to live

Talk to a stranger at night
"It'll be safe"
They never say
Fall in love with a stranger at night
"It'll be a dream"
They tell the world

The hand that once
Held my shoulder in the dark
Is the hand
That lifts my chin
To the light
I am guided by the light
Of the creature who cared for me
May someone also care for you
amen.

Tarantula
Saved my life
He crawled on my arm
Woke me up
Passing by
In the desert
Tarantula
Opened my sandy eyes
To the blaze of the sun
The burning sand
Body shriveling up
Tarantula
Walked my way
I coughed
And kept wandering
Searching for a mirage
To quench my desires

Orange dream
Cactus fiend
Big choices
Total freedom
Beyond belief
Take charge
Move your feet
Being tough
To the moon
Those who teach
Ice cream
Muscle up
You are enough.

Lightning
And the tiger
Were such great friends
Then the lightning
Bit the tiger
They couldn't make amends
Later in time
A star fell down
Humbling the tiger
Into the ground
The thunder cried out
And mourned his friend
Into the sky
They joined again
Lightning in the heavens
Inspired by his stripes
Paint the into black
Scatters the sky
Chasing tiger's back

Forever they play
In the light

And doth my truest nature
Fly on the wings of sparrows
Flutter away
They rapture
For a lovers curse
Is to embark a petty soul
Across the sharp-toothed ocean
To tame the orchard of thine heart
No peasant shall bellow
At the stomach of a lover
Filled with grain and snow

The time is done for sitting around
Now it is time for sitting down
I wouldn't mind all this sitting around
So long as we leave time for sitting down
The leaves pass on from tree to tree
So what's the rush?
Just come sit with me

Socks on my feet
I wonder how they meet
As they squeeze and tire my toes
I look to the floor
And notice the door
That I am supposed to go out
As I wander about
I stop and I shout
Will I ever have the courage to leave?

Please don't hate me
Old friends
And new foe
For there is one thing
That I truly know
I am no cop
At least not anymore
The man who I was
Is not the man who I will be
For the man I am now
Is the sycamore tree
High and mighty
No branches touch the ground
That's where I'll lay my head
And watch the world spin round
There is one thing I must say before I go
The world moves fast
But I move slow

www.ingramcontent.com/pod-product-compliance
Lightning Source LLC
Chambersburg PA
CBHW060422050426
42449CB00009B/2080